Musings

Uzhavi

BookLeaf Publishing

India | USA | UK

Made with ♥ on the BookLeaf Publishing Platform
www.bookleafpub.in
www.bookleafpub.com

Dedication

As I sit down to pen my thoughts, the first thought of how my love for books started come into my mind. It's my cousin, **Dr. M. Kumar,** who was then a college student and I a small, dreamless, aimless, school-goer from a tiny village not known to many. My cousin coming home for his semester holidays brought me a set of books. The glossy shine of pictures, the boldface letters, the smell and feel of something new in my hand, made me sit with them for weeks together. I remember going over those books for weeks together again and again till the point I could verbatim state every word in every page.

Today, when I wish to publish a book, the first person I wish to dedicate it is Dr. M. Kumar for this wonderful journey.

My mother, the only person who can love me for no reason and always praying and wanting me to be someone unique. My beloved husband, my pillar of strength, support, my backbone who just gives nod for any new endeavour I wish to pursue. My son, not just a progeny I brought into this wide world but my replica by many means.

To all my dear friends and students who have loved and encouraged me dearly when I scribble something in the name of Poetry.

This book is a dedication to everyone of them and to the SUPREME, who gave me an intellect that can reflect and pen thoughts. My Salutations and dedications to everyone of the above

Preface

Human mind is always a cluster of thoughts. Why we think, what we think has always remained a mystery. Poetry as it goes without saying, in the words of the legendary William Wordsworth - is a spontaneous overflow of powerful emotions.

Yes, our emotions are always at play. Some vent it in the form of emotions itself, some muse a lot on it and give them a form through their words and pen.

I find poetry as a solace to my own thoughts. I started writing for my own pleasure and when I found that they gave meaning and hope to others, I rejoiced the whole process.

Poetry has so many forms and genres and definitions. But for me it is all about bringing in my thought process as it is, not thinking much about its beauty, rhyme or form.

I started of with blogging, however, wanted to give a solid form to my thoughts and here I have brought out some of my poems that are close to my heart. I just wish and hope, these words can bring you solace too...

Acknowledgements

The followers of my blog, my students, my critics...
Thanks to you all for this amazing journey.

1. ME !!!

How do I define me..
How to understand me..

Sometimes I feel I am like the rain
That's productive, fulfilling and making others gain..
Yet I do detach, shun away and put others through a
strain..

There are times I resemble the air..
Mostly breezy and fair,
And at times utterly stormy & hard to bear.

I do have the patience of the land and let others extract
my love,
Yet I become a fiend
When I no longer can take a blow.

Definitely I become the attractive yet mysterious sky..
Showing very little of me however they try..

I have everything in me and I am a part of everything..
Endlessly giving and never forgiving..
That's what defines me
I am Uniquely different as any one can be...

2. Living the Li(f)e

Quiet and lonely from within
I walked around the mess of my life
People rushing to and from
Wearing a smile hiding their strife

There's smile, frown, anxiety and stress, always on the
run for success
A cocktail of emotions in a constant swirl
Is anyone happy? Everytime I question
Trying to bore through the personality they chose to
present.

One's born and one's gone
In the same minute there's so much to reckon
There's poverty there's abundance
Denying the difference we name that coexistence

Ohh! Let's not talk of the generation gap.
The more you modernise the morer the trap..
Moving from Known strangers to knowing strangers

It's all about living the li(f)e.

The clock keeps ticking, yet time feels still,
In the chaos of life, we chase and we thrill.
But beneath the laughter, a silent plea,
In this crowded silence, please, hear me.

3. House mother...

I wish I were a house mother...
House wife I never wanna be
But mother I sure wish to be

To see my kid wave a bye to school
And eagerly waiting to open the door
Even before his fingers could reach for the bell
But there they're looking for the keys to open the empty
home..
Yes I wish I could be there for him

Needless for him to choose a snack bar a day
Wish I could give him a different cuisine a day
To see that happy face getting all the attention of the
mother..
And cherish the bond forever..
Yes I wish I could be there for him

Not having to make him wait for me
To finish my chores and then attend to his doubts

Not having to shush him when I need to attend an
official call
And giving him the freedom of a home..
Instead here is he shouldering responsibilities and
mothering me...
Oh why can't I be the mother I ought to be.

Mother's are the embodiment of sacrifice we know
But alas the times have changed though
To sacrificing the **"we"** times too..
Oh yeah how I wish I could be a house mother
From being a competitor to him - a frenemy at home

4. My book's My love

What's the best relationship you've ever had...
My friend asked me once..
Immediately I blurted out about my love so divine...
Alas! Surprised was she to know that I had one.

Tell me more she nudged,
I had no choice but to budge..
Unlike any, my love would wait for me,
Without complaining how least I care..
I started to narrate with glee so pure..

I can start afresh,
from wherever I left..
there's nothing more to refresh,
the mind from the complicated mess.

Ageless is my love,
Parting me I would never allow..
Variety she adds to my delight,
With her I find my inner light...

My companion through solitude,
In her presence my heart soars any altitude.
With her I've seen the rise of my life's latitude,
For all the things she's been I owe my gratitude.

She is my twin,
Who gives me escapade from all the din...
She's my kith, she's my kin..
My book's My forever companion.

5. The unheard voice..

If my thoughts had voice
They would scream out loud
Breaking my inhibitions that won't hold
And tell the world what's to be told

But here they're struck in a gaol
As a prisoner of circumstances
Adjudged even without a trial
Crying helplessly for these unusual ventures

Like the baby who yearns to push out of the mother's
womb
They writh and squirm for their way out of this tomb
Yes! Pain or pleasure not given an outlet
Can take away the colours out of life's palette

6. A Clouded mind

My thoughts remained shrouded..
Matching the dark sky that's clouded..
There wasn't air, there wasn't a stir,
But my mind was already in a whir..
Unpleasant memories flashed through sometimes..
Unwanted conversations thundered inside the brain..
Desperately I yearned for a blissful downpour..
To weigh down the heaviness of the darkness so sour..
Slowly a teardrop trickled from within..
Trying to shake away the emotions writhin'..
Like the rain that washes away the impurities around..
My soul's strain found a way out without a sound..
Soon I mellowed and brain became a clear sky..
Radiating the pools of emotions draining into the depths
with a wry..
Oh... tear of the eye or pour of the sky ...
Water's the antidote for any disarray.

7. Confused

The world goes round and round,
Unhindered by any emotional bound,
Then why is it that the human mind,
Is bothered and troubled by the earthly grind
Sometimes this and sometimes that,
Something always pricks and makes us pine,
Why, why and why alone fumes our thoughts,
Making us crumble thinking everything as mine
Oh life is a mirage.. that's absolutely true,
But that's the only hope to hold on to..
Not knowing our worth, or not wanting to find the truth
All days fade of taking away life's mirth.
I hate this grumble, oh! I really do..
But nothing's worthy for me to do
Except the thought of someone's absence
Forgetting all that's present..
Such is life .. oh I realise..
Still not moved nor shaken
From the only hold
That keeps me unbroken

8. Craziness overloaded

Have you ever learnt
To experience silence among chaos
And chaos in silence
Sitting wide awake dreaming
Of a sleep that could calm your being
And sleep just to have a dream that leaves your thoughts
reeling
Oh yes there's hunger and starving
But you can never quench your craving
What can be soothing
You keep wondering
Undeniably this keeps you from all that's thriving
And leaves you to yourself
Coz that's what you feel is truly heartening

9. The working place of devil

In the deep dark corners of my mind
Lies those thoughts dormant
Till I keep myself busy with some or other errand
But when I become imbecile
Oh! How it seethes and reveals it's presence
A Gleeful pain surges through my vein
Putting my personality through a strain
Survival in heat is a challenge
Equally challenging is an avalanche
How tiring are these extremes..
I badly long for some nonchalance
Through the coils of thoughts
One is always lost
Trying to look out
For such is life - we can't assort

10. Why?!

Beep... The call for my day sounded through the neuron..
Tearing me away from my dreamy sojourn like a moron..
Glued were my eyelids to each other
Refusing to let go of one another...
Voluntarily my hand reached out
To extend and give myself a timeout..
But my brain warned me to bate..
Even through the unawakened state
Cursing the alarm starts my everyday..
To do what's needed, putting all thoughts away..
Is it even relevant I wonder a bit!
For the lamp doesn't know why it's being lit...

11. Reminiscences of that night

Oh! That night..
That awful night..
I loved rains and I loved water..
Till that night gave me the dreadful plight..
Whether the darkness enshrouded or the water..
Till date I know not which raised my fear greater..
Oh! those screeching alarms of those water breached
cars!!
With the terrifying blinkers magnifying my horror..
My blank mind reeling with mystic fears.. Of not
knowing the state of the near & dear..
A refugee I was in a stranger's home..
Wishing to see the daylight to come..
Dreadful was that night..
Leaving me with fright...
Forever for darkness and for loss of delight...

12. Rain

Like the thoughts that crawl into an idle mind..
The blue sky blackened with the rainy cloud...
Like a silent intruder the first drop fell.. Giving itself to
the thirsty mud..
The trickle intensified..
Until it draped the sight in view..
Nook & corner the droplets reached.. Leaving a trail of
gleam to mark it's seize. Oh! Rain is a bliss wherever it
fell..
In a shell it becomes a pearl..
While in the ocean it loses it's spell.. Aiding the seed to
sprout with glee.. Filling the pails and the souls of people
for free..
How fulfilling the rain is..
Quenching the thirst of body & soul it's surely a pure
bliss..

13. Oh!! Love it is...

I heard my name and turned around
And met the eyes that reflected my image
Like a camera
My eyes took in the image I saw
And the glimpse got etched in neurons forever..
Oh! into those mysterious caves
That led to a soulful heart
I fell forever..
Stuck like the bee in a candyfloss
Never would I have believed till then
That moments could make hearts go topsy turvy..
That people can go tipsy without getting drunk
That the curve of lips could bridge two souls
Strange is love.. Oh really it is!!!
How else could souls merge when eyes meet..
Wiping off the strangeness and filling life with fragrance
so sweet..

14. That day....

The birds chirped as it dawned..
Mother's began their day's chore
An anonymous stranger smiled at the other..
As usual when he went for his daily stride..
Not knowing that there wouldn't be an office to attend
The dad's of the town rushed out to complete the works
that were on pend
An expectant mother was talking to her bud in the
womb
Thankfully unaware that it would never bloom..
All of them.. Each and every one of them..
Were planning for their happy future..
Unaware that they were building castles in the air..
Every dream of those unknown strangers..
Those beautiful castles of their utopia...
Were just reduced to ashes by that dusty smoke emitting
bastard.. The little boy..

15. Maths 

Every problem has a solution..
Maths says so simply
But every arithmetic puts one into a confusion
If the rules are treated as silly..

Add values says plus
Subtract your ego says minus
Multiply your efforts to make life joyous
And divide the work to avoid being strenuous

Life is not a plane
And we can't go on in a straight line
Curves may take you to top or put you down
Then bend in the proper angle to see your life incline

Yes everything is arithmetic
And arithmetic is everything
So learn it without stress
Never treat maths as mess..

16. Be you

Ohh I do wish to crack down a bit
To see my spirit glow with a lift
From being mechanically perfect
Locking all my fancies away in a closet

My heart nags my neurons
To relish the delights of the day
From the flavour of my chai
To the beauty of the twilight sky.

To stop looking at things for their worth
And appreciate the comfort they bequeath
To remind myself to value my worth
And enjoy every single breath

It's true that glow starts from within
Let's remember loving ourselves is not a sin.

17. A bond forever

How could he have been?
I just wonder
When he was born and made someone's life splendor

I've taken him in arms
And felt his beat & breath
I've seen him smile with charm
And that's the treasure that I can never bequeath

Everything about him I cherish
Times with him is my source of replenish
A grown child he's to me
Forever his cuteness fills me with glee

I just wonder how it will be to mother him
And that bliss is the only thing I miss with him

Will I guide him through storms, teach him to fly?
Hold his dreams close, let him reach for the sky?
With laughter we'll weave a tapestry bright,

In each tender moment, our hearts take flight.

Oh, how the years spin, like stars in the night,
Yet love only deepens, a radiant light.
Together we'll wander, through each twist and turn,
In the warmth of our bond, there's so much to learn.

18. Childhood

Oh! Let's be children forever
Without guile without drama
To be original and natural
Without the worry of being judged
To cry and laugh and be our own self

They blabber they call for attention
They smile and steal away the tension
Their needs are simple and get everything with their
smiling dimple

Everything seems new with them
Learning is fun and there's no boredom
They're the unburdening weight
That can make one feel light

Oh! Let's hold on to the magic they bring,
In the world painted vivid by a child's simple thing.
For time may grow heavy, but in their embrace,
We find the enchantment of love and of grace.

Children the forever pleasure
Childhood is life's greatest treasure

19. Live the life

The umbrella could cover you from drenching
But nothing can stop the touch of the drizzling
Oh you needn't let the waves drag you in
But why go to a beach to not enjoy your feet soaking

You do pluck the Rose knowing the risk of the thorn
You do go to sleep without knowing what might happen
during the night
You do take a challenge knowing that you might fall
You do light a light a lamp knowing it can't last long

People do things coz they wish to do
Knowing that nothing is permanent
Nothing may go as per the plan
It's all about trying and not just about winning...

For in every risk there's a whisper of grace,
In the dance of the rain, find the joy in the chase.
Embrace the uncertainty that life likes to bring,
For even in losses, there's wisdom in suffering.

20. Nature's call

The rustling leaves under the feet
The gentle breeze caressing the body
Chirping birds with their unknown identity
The squirrels hopping from branch to branch

One walks along with nature as one's companion
Starting the day with no hustle-bustle
Slowly taking in and rejoicing the nature at its best
With peace within and glee around

Where did we lose those beautiful times
To the so-called modernity and competive world
Is not the World around to enjoy and slow down?
To be relaxed and live a life worth living

None of the other forms of nature
Has changed what it used to be
It's only our sixth sense that has rendered us senseless
Making us fall for the fallacy as supreme beings.

Let's wake up to the reality
And try to be what we used to be..

27

21. May peace prevail

Ages over ages the wars have not ceased
The reasons differ and so do the plotting
One triumphs and one changes heart
One looses and vanishes leaving behind a history

The war can bring consequences beyond speaking
People may say they won and rejoice the din
But the unquenched fire in their heart
The unspoken feelings become their own hell within

Why then do people fight?
Why not enjoy their fleeting right?
So What if you create history and
be spoken for centuries after you're gone?

No one shall rejoice such a living through ages
People speaking ill of the dead after being gone
May the vitality of youth be spent in better ways
To create a world with peace, harmony and space.

Let laughter be the sword we wield,
Words of kindness, the shield we hold,
Each moment shared, a treasure revealed,
In unity let's weave a World we believe.